A Gift for:

_____

On the Occasion of:

_____

From:

_____

We would like to thank MacKenzie Clark Howard, Ariel Faulkner, and Sandra Lee Clark for their contribution with researching and writing *A Family Advent*.

A Family *Advent*
Copyright © 2008 by Thomas Nelson, Inc.

Published in Nashville, Tennessee, by Thomas Nelson®. Thomas Nelson is a registered trademark of Thomas Nelson, Inc.

Thomas Nelson, Inc. titles may be purchased in bulk for educational, business, fund-raising, or sales promotional use. For information, please e-mail SpecialMarkets@ThomasNelson.com.

Unless otherwise noted, all Scripture references are from *The Holy Bible*, NEW INTERNATIONAL VERSION® © 1973, 1978, 1984 By International Bible Society. Used by permission of Zondervan Publishing House. All rights reserved.

Project Editor: Lisa Stilwell
Designed by Koechel Peterson Design, Minneapolis, MN

ISBN-10: 1–4041–8676–X
ISBN-13: 978–1–4041–8676–7

Printed and bound in China

www.thomasnelson.com

a Family
Advent

THOMAS NELSON
Since 1798

NASHVILLE   DALLAS   MEXICO CITY   RIO DE JANEIRO   BEIJING

This book IS DEDICATED

TO HELPING YOU AND YOURS

grow closer TO OUR LORD AND SAVIOR,

AND *to each other* AT CHRISTMAS.

TABLE OF *Contents*

Introduction

Two thousand years ago in Bethlehem, the world received a very important gift. That's when Jesus first came to earth to walk among us and save us from our sins. And that's what we celebrate every Christmas. For centuries, Christians have anticipated Christmas Day with a month-long observance called Advent.

Advent comes from the Latin *adventus* and means "coming." The main event is the coming, or birth, of Jesus our Savior. As the saints of old anticipated the coming of Christ with great expectation, we, too, eagerly await His return.

The four weeks of Advent, beginning the Sunday nearest November through midnight Christmas Eve, represent the four great "comings" of Christ. The first is His coming in the flesh, His birth, which we celebrate on Christmas Day. The second is His coming into the hearts of all who believe in Him. The third is His coming at the hour of death to the faithful, and the fourth is His coming at the final judgment. To symbolize this progression, Christians use Advent wreaths and candles.

Advent wreaths are attributed to Martin Luther (1483–1546), a German priest who initiated the Protestant Reformation, and they're designed using evergreen branches forming a never-ending circle. The circle and the evergreen branches both symbolize the promise of eternal life through Christ. Four candles (three purple and one pink) are placed on the wreath, representing the four Sundays of Advent. The three purple candles represent penance, and the fourth pink candle is to remind us of the incredible joy that awaits us with the arrival of the Christ child. A fifth candle, generally white and placed in the center of the wreath, is the Christ candle and is lit on Christmas Eve in honor of His birth.

Advent is so much more than a holiday or a tradition of remembrance or memorial; it is a time of spiritual cleansing and growth in Christ. Since the early saints, it has been a time of penitence and fasting, a time of reflection and seeking the Lord. But in current times—in the hustle and bustle of school and church activities, shopping, baking and wrapping—we tend to lose sight of why we do what we do at Christmastime.

It is our hope that this book will help bring you back to a traditional way of worshiping God and celebrating the birth of His Son at Christmas. We hope that in observing these traditions your family will draw closer together and create wonderful new memories and lasting traditions to enjoy year after year. Most of all, we pray this journey brings you deeper, more meaningful communion with our Lord Jesus, the One who came to save us all.

Here is my servant

whom I have chosen, the one
I love, in whom I delight;
I will put my Spirit on him,
and he will proclaim justice to
the nations. . . . In his name
the nations will put their hope."

Matthew 12:18, 21

Hope

Hope is the first topic to
begin our spiritual journey.
Light a purple Advent
candle together as a family.

Sunday

"Do not let your hearts be troubled. Trust in God; trust also in me. In my Father's house are many rooms; if it were not so, I would have told you. I am going there to prepare a place for you. And if I go and prepare a place for you, I will come back and take you to be with me that you also may be where I am."

John 14:1–3

As Christians we have a great reason to hope! John 1:1 proclaims that, "In the beginning was the Word, and the Word was with God, and the Word was God." John 1:14 goes on to say, "The Word became flesh and made his dwelling among us. We have seen his glory, the glory of the One and Only, who came from the Father, full of grace and truth." The Word is Jesus, the living God! We know that everything Scripture tells us is true because it is not only from God, it is God, the Word.

When the prophet Isaiah foretold the birth of Christ, a new hope was born into the world; a hope that lives in us today. And after Jesus came in the flesh, He promised to return and take us to be with Him, giving us eternal hope that surpasses the condition of our life on earth.

Take a moment and talk about the things you want and the things for which you hope—as individuals and as a family. Many of them may be of temporary value, but some will have deep eternal longings as well. Now think and talk about the things you hope for this week, this Christmas season, the new year to come, your lifetime on earth and your next life in heaven. Now ponder in your heart what it will be like to see Jesus face-to-face in all His glory and splendor, and imagine what it will be like to go where He is. Talk about the hope and comfort we have as believers, and that someday Christ will take us home where sin and death have no place.

Your spiritual journey begins the moment you believe in this extraordinary hope, and lasts through all eternity. We invite you to open the Word and open your heart, and begin this day in a deeper relationship with the One and Only, Jesus Christ, our Lord and Savior.

Heavenly Father, we thank You for the blessing of Your Word and Your Son in our lives. We thank You for the hope of our heavenly home where our family can dwell together with You forever. In Christ's name we pray.

Amen.

> "You know the way to the place where I am going."
> Thomas said to him, "Lord, we don't know where
> you are going, so how can we know the way?"
> Jesus answered, "I am the way and the truth and
> the life. No one comes to the Father except through
> me. If you really knew me, you would know
> my Father as well. From now on, you do
> know him and have seen him."
>
> John 14:4–7

Our hope for salvation is in Christ Jesus. He and He alone is the way, the truth and the life. Draw into a closer relationship with Him by reflecting on who He is, His perfect love, His wonderful grace, His tender mercy, His almighty power and majesty. Take a moment to talk about all the blessings in your life for which you are thankful, and praise Jesus for what He has done for you. With Christ living in you, you can celebrate this Christmas and Advent like you never have before!

Dear Jesus, thank You for Your great sacrifice on the cross and the gift of salvation and eternal life. Create in me a pure heart and a desire to really know You. I make this prayer in Jesus' name.

Amen.

Fun fact

You may have noticed that during the Advent season, some churches display the color purple in their sanctuaries, and some display the color blue. And you may have even heard that the color purple is the color of royalty, but do you know why? Well, it all has to do with expensive snails!

Thousands of years ago, when Christ was living on the earth, the color purple was the most expensive dye to produce—only kings could afford such fashionable extravagance. In fact, one ounce of dye (the weight of just five nickels and one penny) cost much more than an entire pound of gold. Why was it so expensive? Believe it or not, the royal dye, called *tekhelet* in Hebrew, was squeezed from snails—a type of mollusk! The extracts were boiled down and mixed with other chemicals to make just the right color. It would take over 10,000 mollusks to make enough dye for just one toga or robe. The process was lost somewhere in the eighth century AD and people throughout history have spent years trying to recreate the dye because of the mystery over whether it was purple or blue.

In ancient documents, the color *tekhelet* is often described as violet, but other sources refer to it as the same color as the sky or sea, which would mean it was blue. Even today, scientists are analyzing biological, chemical and archaeological data to try and figure it out, but no one has been able to find an answer. Regardless of whether your church chooses to use purple or royal blue in the weeks leading up to Christmas, the meaning is the same. During Advent we prepare the way and honor Christ the Lord, the one true King, with the most royal color we can find.

Tuesday

Philip said, "Lord, show us the Father and that will be enough for us." Jesus answered: "Don't you know me, Philip, even after I have been among you such a long time? Anyone who has seen me has seen the Father. How can you say, 'Show us the Father'? Don't you believe that I am in the Father, and that the Father is in me? The words I say to you are not just my own. Rather, it is the Father, living in me, who is doing his work. Believe me when I say that I am in the Father and the Father is in me; or at least believe on the evidence of the miracles themselves. I tell you the truth, anyone who has faith in me will do what I have been doing. He will do even greater things than these, because I am going to the Father. And I will do whatever you ask in my name, so that the Son may bring glory to the Father. You may ask me for anything in my name, and I will do it."

John 14:8–14

The New Testament has many examples of Christ's wondrous miracles. He healed the sick, raised the dead, and fed thousands, yet He tells us that we can go on to do even greater deeds through His Spirit. Ask God how He wants to use you this Christmas. Maybe you will feed the homeless in your community, clothe the poor, or bring comfort to the sick and lonely. If you ask for His guidance, He will work through you and direct your path. Even the smallest act of grace can change a life, a community, and even the world.

The hope we have as Christians is not only that we have Christ living in us, but also that we have Him working through us. Hope teaches us to have faith in Christ and to do the things He leads us to do. Acting under the power of Christ will produce amazing results.

Dear Lord,

please show us how You
would have us serve others
this Christmas season,
and empower us as
Your vessels that, by
serving others, we
may bring You glory.
We thank You and praise
You and ask these things
in Your Son's name.

Amen.

ACTIVITY
THE NIGHT SKY

What You'll Need:
❄ a star map
(you can buy one or print one off the Web; SkyandTelescope.com is a good place to start)
❄ a clear night sky

One of the most beautiful creations God left for us here on earth is the night sky. So for today's family activity, we're going to take a very close look at it by stargazing! (If it's a cloudy evening, make sure you plan for the next clear night.)

For centuries, stars have been used as a compass to guide people in their travels. In the United States, African American slaves used to look to the Big Dipper to point them north toward freedom. Can you think of a group of people we talk about during Advent who used the stars too? If you said the Magi or Wise Men you are right on the mark, and we'll learn some more about them a little later in this book.

You can look at the stars by just going out into your backyard or a safe park. Wherever you go, it's best to be away from lights so, if you live in the city, it's a good idea to find a more rural location in order to have the best view. It takes a half an hour for your eyes to fully adjust to the dark and see the most stars, so make sure you bring plenty of blankets and clothing for bundling up. But before you set out on your stargazing adventure, be sure to study your star map so you can be prepared to find specific groups of stars called constellations.

Some constellations are circumpolar, which means that they never rise or set and the only reason we can't see them during the day is because of the sun, but they're there all the time. Others are seasonal constellations that change throughout the year meaning you can see some during the fall, but not in the spring, and others during the spring, but not in the fall. All stars fall into either of these categories except for one very special star that the Magi saw. The Gospel of Matthew tells us the Wise Men observed a new star rising for the very first time in the East, which marked the birth of the Messiah and led them to Bethlehem (2:2). While you're out stargazing, imagine you are one of the Wise Men and see if you can find a star bright enough to guide you hundreds of miles to seek out a King!

Wednesday

"If you love me, you will obey what I command. And I will ask the Father, and he will give you another Counselor to be with you forever—the Spirit of truth. The world cannot accept him, because it neither sees him nor knows him. But you know him, for he lives with you and will be in you. I will not leave you as orphans; I will come to you. Before long, the world will not see me anymore, but you will see me. Because I live, you also will live. On that day you will realize that I am in my Father, and you are in me, and I am in you."

John 14:15–20

Take time to really think about these words: Jesus is in the Father and we are in Jesus and He is in us. How incredible it is that we have the Lord God in us and we are in Him! Acts 17:28 describes this mystery in this way: "For in Him we live and move and have our being."

How often do we really live moment-by-moment in Christ? Imagine how much better our busy days would be if we practiced the presence of Jesus. Each year at Christmastime we say that we are going to slow down, cut back on activities, and enjoy the season, but somehow it never seems to happen. Instead, we need to make a commitment to live daily in Christ. Then, whatever the task, the event, or the circumstance, He will enrich our lives in ways that are beyond imagination. This ultimate relationship with Christ is above all others; it will guide us on our spiritual journey and last through all eternity.

Dear Christ Jesus,

help us to daily abide in You.
We want to experience
this mystery—living in You,
and You in us. Help us to
pause and practice the
presence of the Lord this
Christmas. We make this
prayer in Your holy name.

Amen.

Did you know?

The season of Advent has always been connected to the promise of hope, but it hasn't always been a celebration. It used to be that every year at the Feast of the Epiphany, the day we now know as Three Kings Day on the 6th of January, all of the people who converted to Christianity within the previous year were then baptized. The weeks leading up to this day were spent as a time of fasting and penitence, each person asking God to forgive their sins. The church realized that the Old Testament emphasized a different sentiment. It does not anticipate the coming of the Messiah with remembering personal sins, but it celebrates His arrival as relief from the darkness, delivering us into the light. The Bible tells us to be joyful as we wait for Christ to arrive, and so today that is just what we do. To make it even more of a celebration, the Church decided in the ninth century that the first Sunday of Advent would mark the beginning of the entire Church calendar. This means that every first Sunday of Advent begins our spiritual journey for the whole year to come.

Thursday

"Whoever has my commands and obeys them, he is the one who loves me. He who loves me will be loved by my Father, and I too will love him and show myself to him." Then Judas (not Judas Iscariot) said, "But, Lord, why do you intend to show yourself to us and not to the world?" Jesus replied, "If anyone loves me, he will obey my teaching. My Father will love him, and we will come to him and make our home with him. He who does not love me will not obey my teaching. These words you hear are not my own; they belong to the Father who sent me."

John 14:21–24

What an awesome hope; in our time, study, prayer, and obedience to the Word, Jesus will reveal himself to us and lead us into a deeper relationship with Him. We are simply to obey. As parents, we teach our children to obey because we want them to be safe and secure. In the same way, our heavenly Father asks us to follow His will. Obedience is a positive thing. When God prompts us to do or not do something, remember that blessings will surely follow if we're obedient. The quicker we act out His will, the sooner we will be blessed. Obey the Lord's commands and you'll abide in the love of the Father, and the Son, and the Holy Spirit.

Dear Heavenly Father,

help us to know You more and to be obedient to You in all things that we may bring glory to Your name. We make this request in Christ's name. *Amen.*

ACTIVITY
THE GIVING HEART

What You'll Need:
❄ a giving heart

You've probably *grown* quite a bit over the past year, so its time to sort through all your clothes and toys and weed out what you don't wear or play with anymore. There are lots of kids just like you all over the world who don't have many nice things, so why not spread a little Christmas joy? Being selfless and giving during Advent is a perfect way to celebrate the beautiful gifts we've received from God. Get your parents involved, too, because there are probably things sitting in their closets and cupboards that they don't use anymore. There are dozens of organizations that help manage donations, including Toys for Tots www.toysfortots.org and Goodwill www.goodwill.org. Be sure to check if your church has a connection with one charity in particular and start cleaning out those closets!

"All this I have spoken while still with you. But the Counselor, the Holy Spirit, whom the Father will send in my name, will teach you all things and will remind you of everything I have said to you. Peace I leave with you; my peace I give you. I do not give to you as the world gives. Do not let your hearts be troubled and do not be afraid."

John 14:25–27

As Christians we are not immune to trials and hard times, but when we are burdened and afraid we have hope in the Lord and comfort from the Holy Spirit. When our external lives are full of turmoil, we tend to spend more time on our knees in prayer; this leads to a greater dependence on God. And though God does not cause bad things to happen to us, He sometimes allows them so we will grow closer to Him and learn to trust Him more. Release your troubled heart to the Lord and He will give you peace. He will teach you to abide in Him and share in a peaceful communion that is true and lasting. He has promised and has said, "Never will I leave you; never will I forsake you" Hebrews 14:5. Hope and know that internally, within our very souls, we can always find peace in the Lord.

Dear Jesus,

we turn over our troubled hearts and burdens to You this day and receive Your hope and peace. In the precious name of Jesus we pray.

Amen.

TIME MACHINE

CLIMB ON IN and buckle up, folks.

Welcome aboard our time machine! Make sure you hang on tight, because we're racing back thousands of years! Uh oh! We just bumped into Elvis and now we're taking a left at the signing of the Declaration of Independence and a right toward the Mayflower sailing on the Atlantic. Cities and populations are decreasing—towns are moving farther apart and some are even disappearing. Wow! We just passed by a little village called Bethlehem, but we're not ready to stop yet! Hey, we just flew by a gladiator—watch out for that sword! Whew! We made it.

Ladies and gentlemen, welcome to Ancient Greece. By now you're probably wondering why our trusty time machine brought us to this particular place. Well, it all has to do with words. Words, words, words. Much too often we take words for granted. For example, what would we be without the word *pasta*? We'd be hungry, that's what! Now what about the word *Advent*? We've certainly already used it a lot in this book , and we know it's an important part of every year, but what about the word itself? The word *Advent* originally came from the Greek word *parousia* meaning *presence*. Well, that makes sense doesn't it? The presence of Christ. Now fast forward a few thousand years and we find the Latin word *adventus* meaning *a coming*. Now we not only have the presence of the Lord on earth but an understanding of his *adventus*, his arrival. The first time the word *Advent* appeared in the English language was in 1099 AD—over a thousand years after the death of Jesus. An ancient document included in what's known as the Saxon Chronicles reads, *"Osmond biscop of Searbyrið innon Aduent forðferde."* Now, not many people can understand Old English or even recognize some of those letters, but I bet you can see that word *Aduent*, which became *Advent* as we know it today. Thousands of years before the coming of Jesus Christ, God was planting the seeds of these words so that when He did come, we would recognize the realization of the prophecy of His coming, and know exactly how to spread the news about His arrival. So, just as the word *pasta* helps us avoid being hungry, the word *Advent* helps us make room for the greatest fulfillment of all.

"You heard me say, 'I am going away and I am coming back to you.' If you loved me, you would be glad that I am going to the Father, for the Father is greater than I. I have told you now before it happens, so that when it does happen you will believe. I will not speak with you much longer, for the prince of this world is coming. He has no hold on me, but the world must learn that I love the Father and that I do exactly what my Father has commanded me. Come now; let us leave."

John 14:28–31

Jesus has given us tremendous hope in Him, in the Father, and in the Holy Spirit. He has gone away for a time, but He is coming back—He promised! While we are here on this earth and for all of eternity, we have fellowship in Christ through the Holy Spirit.

May your spiritual journey lead you to abide in Christ and to obey His teaching. May you spread the hope and love of Christ this Christmas season as you share Him with others. And may you put your faith into action as you give of yourself, your time, and your talents. Finally, we invite you to rejoice and celebrate in the greatest Hope the world has ever been offered.

Dear Savior,

live in us and enable us to share the hope of Christ through encouraging words and actions this Advent season and throughout our lives. We make this prayer in Your name. *Amen.*

ACTIVITY

Get *Involved* in a *Charity*

There are many opportunities to get involved with charities in the weeks leading up to Christmas, including ones that help kids and families. Christ entered the world as a vulnerable child, teaching us that every child is a blessing and is someone for whom we must care. Angel Tree is a wonderful way to deliver the gift of love and hope to children who have parents in prison. The cost is minimal and you have the opportunity to deliver your gifts in person. For more information please visit www.angeltree.org. You can also find out what your church is doing to help people in the community, or contact your local social services to see if you can adopt a family for Christmas or help in other ways. Remember, too, that our blessings can be shared throughout the year as well. An organization such as the Make-a-Wish Foundation (www.wish.org) helps to make dreams come true for children with life-threatening medical conditions. Go on the Web site, read the stories, and learn how you can share the power of granting a wish.

Glory to God in the highest,

and on earth peace to men

on whom his favor rests. "

Luke 2:14

Peace

Peace is the second topic of our spiritual journey. Light the first two purple Advent candles together as a family.

Sunday

> For to us a child is born, to us a son is given,
> and the government will be on his shoulders.
> And he will be called Wonderful Counselor,
> Mighty God, Everlasting Father, Prince of Peace.
>
> Isaiah 9:6

Peace is one of the greatest gifts the Lord has brought to us. In the verse above, the prophet Isaiah helps us to recognize the peace we will have upon Christ's arrival, and goes on to proclaim the glory and majesty of who He is and His purpose for coming.

Wonderful Counselor points to the Messiah as King—a king who will direct and guide, and carry out a plan of action—but also One the world will know as loving and compassionate; One who cares about each and every one of us and the smallest details of our lives.

Mighty God refers to His divine power. He spoke, and the earth, sun, moon and stars came into being. He parted the seas, stopped the waves, and performed miracles that we talk about to this very day.

Everlasting Father indicates that His grace and mercy are never ending, and that He will never leave us or forsake us. Ever.

Prince of Peace reminds us that only through Jesus Christ we will have true peace of mind and soul. Faith in Christ brings peace with the Father, and it is on believers that God's favor of peace will rest.

Take a moment now to discuss and think about these elements of God's nature, and why we have peace in His completeness.

Wonderful Counselor,

Mighty God, Everlasting Father, Prince of Peace, we praise You for Your glory and majesty this day and always. We thank You for Your comfort, guidance, and provision. May we be ever mindful of who You are. We make this prayer in Jesus' name. *Amen.*

Monday

> Rejoice in the Lord always, I will say it again: Rejoice! Let your gentleness be evident to all. The Lord is near. Do not be anxious about anything, but in everything, by prayer and petition, with thanksgiving, present your requests to God. And the peace of God, which transcends all understanding, will guard your hearts and your minds in Christ Jesus.
>
> Philippians 4:4–7

Prayer connects us to the Father in an intimate communion of heart, soul, and spirit—it is a mysterious dialogue of love and power with a most Holy God. And Jesus is our faithful intercessor—our heavenly ambassador who presents our prayers to God. Through prayer, God's power is released to work in your life and the lives of others, bringing peace and comfort in knowing He has heard you and will answer you in His time.

When you present your requests to God, do so in humble submission with thanksgiving in your heart. The Lord will then guard your heart and mind with peace that transcends all understanding.

Heavenly Father,

we ask this day that Your hand be upon our nation and all of the nations on earth. Please guide our president, the leaders of our country, and leaders around the world, from the smallest of towns to our global communities. We lift up the wars that are raging now, and we ask for peace for all who are affected by them. We ask that You bless soldiers and their families, our missionaries, our pastors, friends, and our families. Please bless the hungry, the sick, and the lonely. Thank You that Your love, grace, and peace are available to all the people of the world. In Jesus' name we pray. *Amen.*

Fun fact

Evergreen seem to sprout up everywhere during Advent and Christmas. Think about how many wreaths, trees, and decorations you see each day—it's probably quite a lot! So why is that? What's so special about evergreen? Evergreen is the name we give to certain types of plants and trees. They are unique because they are forever green all year long, even in the middle of winter when most other plants are dormant.

There are many different kinds of evergreen we can use to make an Advent wreath, and they each have different meanings. Laurel represents victory over persecution and suffering; pine and yew symbolize immortality; cedar stands for strength and healing; and holly, with its prickliness, reminds us of the crown of thorns that Jesus wore when He died on the cross. One or all of these ever-green elements can be used to make your wreath.

It's also important to know that the shape of the Advent wreath has just as much meaning as the materials we use. A circle that has no end and no beginning symbolizes God's eternal love for us and His gift of everlasting life.

Do you have any evergreen in your house? If you have a Christmas tree, then you definitely do—probably pine, spruce, or fir, which are the most common varieties. Did you know that Christmas trees have a special story, just like the Advent wreath? There is a legend about a man from the eighth century named Saint Boniface, who was traveling as a missionary in Germany. The story is that one day Saint Boniface stumbled upon a group of pagans worshiping an old oak tree in the middle of a forest. He chopped down the tree to show them that it wasn't a god but rather a false idol, and that there is only one true God to worship. Over time, a fir tree grew in place of the oak tree and was designated the very first Christmas tree. Eventually, the pagans came to understand the one true God everlasting—ever-green with life and hope—and they became followers of Christ. Now every time you see an evergreen tree or wreath, you'll know that it means God is with us for all eternity, guiding us through the dark of winter with the promise of everlasting life.

Let the peace of Christ rule in your hearts, since as members of one body you were called to peace. And be thankful. Let the word of Christ dwell in you richly as you teach and admonish one another with all wisdom, and as you sing psalms, hymns and spiritual songs with gratitude in your hearts to God. And whatever you do, whether in word or deed, do it all in the name of the Lord Jesus, giving thanks to God the Father through him.

Colossians 3:15–17

On any given day, we experience many emotions. And sometimes those emotions will try to rule our hearts. This happens when we spend too much time being anxious, angry, depressed, or fearful. But the good news is, we have the power within us to choose between letting our emotions rule within us, or letting the Prince of Peace flood our soul with tranquility and thankfulness.

When people watch us apply the power we're promised in God's Word, we have a much better chance of reaching them with Christ's love. Your family, friends, and co-workers see what you're going through in your life, sometimes on a daily basis. How you handle yourself and your emotions can make a great impact for Christ.

Dear Heavenly Father,
thank You for giving us emotions. Help us to control them in a way that allows Your peace to rule over them all, so that we might be a light of love to everyone around us. We make this prayer in Christ's name. *Amen.*

ACTIVITY

What You'll Need:
❊ a piece of paper
❊ a pen

WHICH NATIVITY CHARACTER ARE YOU?

This book is all about getting ready for Christmas Day and, as it approaches, we thought it would be fun to take a quiz to see what nativity character you have most in common with. After you answer the following questions, you can check your results on page 44.

How are you most likely to spend your summer?
   a. Traveling
   b. At home with your family
   c. Hanging out at your friends' houses
   d. Earning money with babysitting, mowing lawns, etc.

What's your favorite part of the school day?
   a. English or Science
   b. Gym
   c. Recess or Lunch
   d. Math

Which is most like you?
   a. An owl
   b. A dog
   c. A butterfly
   d. A cat

What is your favorite light in the dark?
   a. The stars
   b. A campfire
   c. A room full of candles
   d. A black light

One day you're ideal job will involve:
   a. Learning more than your brain can hold
   b. Helping a lot of people
   c. Meeting all kinds of different people
   d. Being really busy and doing well

Which of these is most important to you?
   a. Books
   b. Pets
   c. Phone
   d. Money

Which of the following is your favorite holiday?
   a. The Fourth of July: a little history and an amazing parade
   b. Thanksgiving: a big meal around the dining room table
   c. Halloween: costumes and candy galore
   d. New Year's Eve: the biggest party of the year

43

Your biggest weakness is that sometimes you can be:

   a. A know-it-all

   b. Shy

   c. Loud

   d. Bossy

Where would you rather live?

   a. In a foreign country

   b. The house you grew up in

   c. A brand new neighborhood with lots of families

   d. A big city

If you saw something unbelievable, what would you do first?

   a. Find out how it happened

   b. Try to get closer

   c. Tell someone about it

   d. Sell tickets

Whichever letter you scored the most determines with Nativity character you are! Share your results with each of your family members and talk about how many different kinds of people it takes to complete just one part of a beautiful story—the birth of Christ.

If you answered mostly As then you're a MAGI.

That's right! You're most like the wise Magi. You love to learn new things and are curious about the world around you. Traveling to new places, trying new kinds of food, and reading plenty of good books are some of your favorite activities. Someday you'll help lots of people understand all that you've discovered, and maybe even have time for a little star gazing. But you're so clever, you probably already figured that out!

If you answered mostly Bs then you're a SHEPHERD.

Congratulations! You're about as loyal as a person can get. You love animals and being out in nature where life is nice and simple. Taking care of your family and your small group of close friends is very important to you. In the future you'll be the person everyone goes to when they're feeling a bit down because you make everyone feel special and safe. Take care of that flock!

If you answered mostly Cs then you're an ANGEL.

You are quite the social butterfly! You light up a room with all your stories. You spend lots of time talking to your friends—whether online, on the phone, or in person. Chances are you have a great smile and people like being around you. Someday you could have an excellent career in communications, acting as a heavenly herald every day of the year! Spread those wings and fly….

If you answered mostly Ds then you're an INNKEEPER.

Now, you're probably thinking this doesn't sound like you, but wait! This is one of the most important roles in the Nativity story and in life itself. People like you make the world go round because you've got a head for business. You understand how to organize people to work together. In essence, you're a good leader and an independent thinker. But you also help people out by providing security and protection to anyone who comes knocking on your door. One day you'll probably be in charge of a lot of people, but they'll know your good heart and will always trust you.

Wednesday

Finally, all of you, live in harmony with one another; be sympathetic, love as brothers, be compassionate and humble. Do not repay evil with evil or insult with insult, but with blessing, because to this you were called so that you may inherit a blessing. For, "Whoever would love life and see good days must keep his tongue from evil and his lips from deceitful speech. He must turn from evil and do good; he must seek peace and pursue it. For the eyes of the Lord are on the righteous and his ears are attentive to their prayer."

1 Peter 3:8–12

What is the definition of peace? Webster's New World Dictionary defines it as freedom from war; a state of harmony, serenity, or quiet. The Bible says we are to seek the Lord with all our hearts and in return, He will give us peace that passes all understanding (Philippians 4:7). The peace we receive from knowing the Lord extends far beyond our outward circumstances—even when we are not in a state of harmony—going directly into our heart, soul, and mind. It is a peace that enables us to live in harmony with one another, to love as brothers, and to be compassionate and humble. And because of this gift, we are able to do good deeds and show sincere love to others from the overflow of this wonderful peace.

Dear Jesus,

make our hearts desire to seek You and Your peace, that we may do good and inherit Your blessings. We make this prayer in Your name. *Amen.*

Did you know?

Did you know that Santa Claus was really a Christian saint named Saint Nicholas? Who lived just three hundred years after the death of Christ? You'll have to decide whether you think he wore a big red suit or not, but there's a good reason why we mention him at Christmastime. Saint Nicholas was born into a very wealthy family in Greece. His parents died when he was very young and he spent the rest of his life giving away every bit of his inheritance in Christian charity. He particularly loved children and became known as a miracle worker. One legend tells the story of a father who was too poor to give his three daughters a dowry. Not having a dowry meant the daughters probably wouldn't find husbands, and if they didn't marry, they'd be sold into slavery! Mysteriously, on three different nights over the years, Saint Nicholas tossed a bag of gold through an open window into the poor man's house, and each time it landed in the girls' stockings, which were hanging by the fire to dry. So the daughters ended up being able to find husbands, and the tradition of hanging stockings began. And since that time, Saint Nicholas became known as a giver of gifts.

Saint Nicholas died in 343 AD, but that didn't stop the miracles from happening. The people whose lives had been changed by this humble follower of Christ declared December 6th as the feast of Saint Nicholas, and each year, on the eve of that day, they would throw candies and small gifts through the doors of their neighbors' houses. Children in Holland started leaving carrots and hay in their shoes for the saint's horse, hoping the spirit of Saint Nicholas would leave them small gifts in exchange.

So how did Saint Nicholas' name change to Santa Claus? The German pronunciation of Saint Nicholas is *Sankt Niklaus*, which got a little mixed up and became Santa Claus as the legend got passed on through the generations. Whether you like to think of Santa Claus as a man in a big red suit or a saint who lived long ago doesn't really matter. What's important is that we recognize his example of true giving and faithfulness in the way that Jesus teaches us. Maybe this Christmas you can help spread the spirit of Saint Nicholas and leave a caring surprise at someone's door or mailbox.

Those who live according to the sinful nature have their minds set on what that nature desires; but those who live in accordance with the Spirit have their minds set on what the Spirit desires. The mind of sinful man is death, but the mind controlled by the Spirit is life and peace; the sinful mind is hostile to God. It does not submit to God's law, nor can it do so. Those controlled by the sinful nature cannot please God. You, however, are controlled not by the sinful nature but by the Spirit, if the Spirit of God lives in you. And if anyone does not have the Spirit of Christ, he does not belong to Christ. But if Christ is in you, your body is dead because of sin, yet your spirit is alive because of righteousness. And if the Spirit of him who raised Jesus from the dead is living in you, he who raised Christ from the dead will also give life to your mortal bodies through his Spirit, who lives in you.

Romans 8:5–11

We now know we are to move beyond our emotions and seek peace through prayer and meditation; the challenge now is to keep our minds steadfast on what the Spirit desires. Our sinful nature is constantly at war with the Spirit. But Christ living in us gives us victory over that war, enabling us to live in righteousness. Day by day, moment by moment we can choose to live by the Spirit, resulting in the presence of His peace. And just as Christ's body was raised from the dead, our bodies will also rise because of the indwelling presence of the Spirit.

Dear Lord,

we pray for the indwelling of the Spirit of Christ that gives life and peace and the promised resurrection. In your Son's name we pray.

Amen.

ACTIVITY

Oatmeal Christmas Cookies

What you'll need:

1 cup butter, softened
1 cup brown sugar, packed
½ cup granulated sugar
2 eggs
1 teaspoon vanilla
1½ cups all-purpose flour
1 teaspoon baking soda

1 teaspoon ground cinnamon
½ teaspoon ground cloves *(optional)*
½ teaspoon salt
3 cups rolled oats
1 cup M&Ms®
Hungry bellies
Helping Hands

It's time to have a family bake night!

Preheat oven to 350°. In a large bowl, cream together the butter, brown sugar, granulated sugar, eggs, and vanilla until smooth. Combine the flour, baking soda, cinnamon, cloves, and salt; stir into the sugar mixture. Stir in the rolled oats and M&Ms® with a wooden spoon.

Drop dough by rounded teaspoons, two inches apart onto an ungreased cookie sheet.

Bake 10–12 minutes until light and golden. Remove from the oven and let the cookies cool on the cookie sheet for two minutes. Transfer to a wire rack and let cool completely. Store in airtight container.

These are best enjoyed with milk or hot cocoa while curled up watching an old Christmas movie! Just make sure you save a batch to share for this weekend's activity!

Do not put out the Spirit's fire; do not treat prophecies with contempt. Test everything. Hold on to the good. Avoid every kind of evil. May God himself, the God of peace, sanctify you through and through. May your whole spirit, soul and body be kept blameless at the coming of our Lord Jesus Christ. The one who calls you is faithful and he will do it.

1 Thessalonians 5:19–24

The baby in the manger teaches us one very important thing: that God cares about us and wants to change our lives. And when He works in the lives of His people, we see love, faithfulness, righteousness, and peace. As you worship this Advent, open your heart, your mind, your body, and your soul, and find calm within. Then, in that quiet moment, the Spirit's fire will fill you. That warm glow of His passion and presence is how you know God is making you into a brand-new person.

Our transformation into godly people depends on who God is and how He works in us. Second Corinthians 3:18 says, "And we, who with unveiled faces all reflect the Lord's glory, are being transformed into his likeness with ever-increasing glory, which comes from the Lord, who is the Spirit." Let the peace of God's presence transform you today and every day.

Dear Christ Jesus,
begin Your transforming work
in our lives, sanctify us,
and carry out Your plans for
us until Your return and
the arrival of eternal peace.
We make this prayer
in Your holy name. *Amen.*

TIME MACHINE

CLIMB ABOARD

and buckle up, folks! We're in for a bumpy ride. The time machine is taking us back to an age before computers, hair dryers, or video games; before running water, electricity, or air conditioning, and waaaay before cell phones. Hey, can someone turn on a flashlight? Without electricity it's getting awfully dark out there. We're even further back in time from where we stopped on our last time machine trip, and things are looking awfully desert-y. Hey, watch out for the huge cat! Oh, wait . . . oops . . . this is where we're supposed to land! Welcome to Ancient Egypt, ladies and gentlemen. And, in case you're wondering, that huge cat is actually the Sphinx.

We've come all this way to find out about . . . candles! Even though we have electricity, we still use candles—bet you have some in your house right now—but they're especially important to the Advent wreath. Let's check it out.

The Egyptians were the first people to make small torches by soaking reeds in molten tallow, which is basically melted animal fat. Pretty gross stuff, and it doesn't smell so great either! Now if you fast-forward a millennium or so to the Middle Ages, people were trying to find a quicker and easier way to make the torches (or candles) because they needed a lot of them—for everything from street lamps to candlelight for reading or sewing. Can you imagine walking down the street or reading a book without light? People tried everything: beeswax, bayberries, and even whale oil. To make the candles, they'd take a tiny braided rope (the wick) and dip it into a pot of melted liquid hundreds of times. It would take hours to make just a few candles. Then in 1879 the light bulb was invented and candles weren't needed for light anymore, but we still use them to symbolize celebration and define a time of ceremony, like when we light the Advent wreath.

For thousands of years people have tried to create and sustain light using candles. Light is something we need to see where we are going. We don't use candles in our practical lives anymore, but we certainly need them on our spiritual journey. Candles help us understand the way to God, who is the eternal light and life.

Saturday

May the God of peace, who through the blood
of the eternal covenant brought back from
the dead our Lord Jesus, that great Shepherd
of the sheep, equip you with everything good
for doing his will, and may he work in us
what is pleasing to him, through Jesus Christ,
to whom be glory for ever and ever. Amen.

Hebrews 13:20–21

The Christmas season comes and goes so fast—one minute you're eating Thanksgiving dinner, the next you're boxing up the tree. But the peace we have with God isn't just a feeling that will pass in time. Our peace comes from living with God, and Him living in us, all year round. Because Christ came and died to forgive our sins, we get to have a one-on-one relationship with Him. He equips us with everything good, like love, grace, mercy, faith, faithfulness, obedience, and perseverance, and if we keep walking with Him and developing those traits, we'll grow in Him and become more and more able to carry out His will.

May your confidence in the hope of God's glory—and the peace that comes with it—be steadfast and strong. May the purpose for which God created you be fulfilled, and may you grow to be all that He intended.

Dear Savior, we thank You, Lord, for the shedding of Your blood that puts us in a right relationship with the God of peace. We praise You for equipping us with everything good for doing His will and working in us what is pleasing to God. In Your name we make this prayer. *Amen.*

ACTIVITY

We all like to feel *noticed.*

There's just something *special* about

hearing someone call you by name

and ask you how you are.

Do you know the name of your mail carrier? Newspaper deliverer? School crossing

guard? As a family, take the time to learn the names of the people who serve you every

day. You can make someone's day by introducing yourself and telling them how much

you appreciate their work. For something extra special, bundle up some of those cookies

you made this week and give them a yummy Christmas treat! (Kids, please remember

to never talk to strangers without Mom and Dad with you!)

The LORD appeared

to us in the past, saying:
"I have loved you with an
everlasting love; I have drawn
you with loving-kindness."

Jeremiah 31:3

Love

Continuing on your journey,
light the three purple Advent
candles together as a family.

"For God so loved the world that he gave his one and only Son, that whoever believes in him shall not perish but have eternal life. For God did not send his Son into the world to condemn the world, but to save the world through him. Whoever believes in him is not condemned, but whoever does not believe stands condemned already because he has not believed in the name of God's one and only Son."

John 3:16–18

God's wonderful plan of salvation was motivated by His great love for us. He desires to have an intimate relationship with us now, and for us to be with Him for all eternity. That's why Jesus was born in a manger and died on the cross: to provide a way for us to reach the Father.

To receive this gift of salvation, all we have to do is believe and receive. Now, believing is not based on how we feel. Believing is a response to God's truth. And we act out our belief by making the decision to turn from our sins and receive God's forgiveness.

Believing in Jesus as God's Son, in His sacrificial death on the cross, and in His resurrection promises us something amazing: salvation and eternal life. God's infinite love for us has provided a way for us to be with Him forever. And that's definitely something to celebrate!

Dear Heavenly Father,
we thank You for Your great love and for making Your salvation available to all of mankind, given to all who believe in and receive it. In Christ's name we pray. *Amen.*

Monday

How great is the love the Father has lavished
on us, that we should be called children of God!
And that is what we are! The reason the world does
not know us is that it did not know him.
Dear friends, now we are children of God, and what
we will be has not yet been made known. But we
know that when he appears, we shall be like him,
for we shall see him as he is. Everyone who has this
hope in him purifies himself, just as he is pure.

1 John 3:1–3

The Christmas season has a way of reminding us of how great family can

be. But did you know that one of God's greatest gifts—and it's a gift of grace,

not something we could achieve on our own—is becoming a member of His

own family? And as wonderful as it is to have an earthly mom and dad and brothers and sisters who care about us, it's an even greater honor and joy to be included in God's holy family.

With Him as our heavenly Father, we are united with all our fellow believers. Just imagine all of the Christians in your church being part of your family. Now imagine how many believers there are in your state, your country, the world, and from all generations and all time. The truth is that all of us are one family, connected by the love of God.

Jesus is coming back again, and when He appears we shall see Him, we shall be like Him, and we shall worship Him with our brothers and sisters in faith forever. Let's thank God for the gift of an eternal family!

Dear Jesus, thank You for making us part of Your family and for teaching us to look forward to Your appearing. In Your name we make this prayer. *Amen.*

Fun fact

Did you know that during Bible times, shepherds were often considered outcasts in society? They couldn't participate in religious ceremonies, for example, because they were considered "unclean." They were generally the poor peasants of their day and were often suspected of being thieves.

Isn't it amazing to the think that God chose these people to be the first to hear the good news about Jesus? Of all the people in the world, of all the kings and people with wealth and power, or even just the regular folks, God chose to send His mighty angels to the shepherds—the outcasts—and allow them to greet the Christ child.

No matter what you may think about yourself, or what others may think about you, God loves you so much that He sent His own Son, Jesus, just for you. Even if you were the only person on the earth, even if you were a thief or a smelly shepherd, God would have sent Jesus just for you. This Christmas and Advent, respond just as the shepherds did: run to Jesus, and tell everyone what you have seen!

Tuesday

For this reason I kneel before the Father, from whom his whole family in heaven and on earth derives its name. I pray that out of his glorious riches he may strengthen you with power through his Spirit in your inner being, so that Christ may dwell in your hearts through faith. And I pray that you, being rooted and established in love, may have power, together with all the saints, to grasp how wide and long and high and deep is the love of Christ, and to know this love that surpasses knowledge—that you may be filled to the measure of all the fullness of God. Now to him who is able to do immeasurably more than all we ask or imagine, according to his power that is at work within us, to him be glory in the church and in Christ Jesus throughout all generations, for ever and ever! Amen.

Ephesians 3:14–21

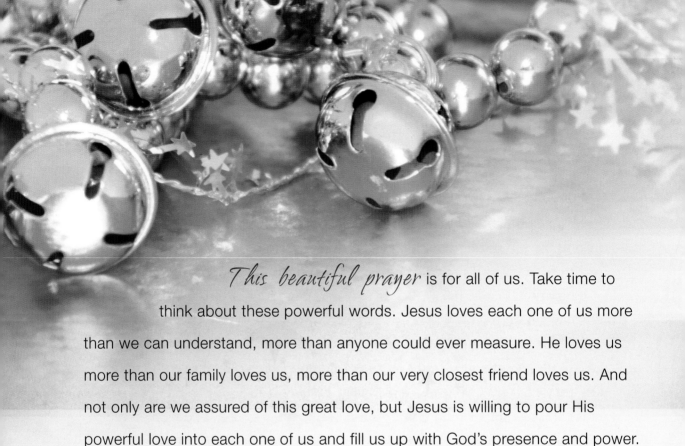

This beautiful prayer is for all of us. Take time to think about these powerful words. Jesus loves each one of us more than we can understand, more than anyone could ever measure. He loves us more than our family loves us, more than our very closest friend loves us. And not only are we assured of this great love, but Jesus is willing to pour His powerful love into each one of us and fill us up with God's presence and power.

Now imagine this power is at work in you. What will you do for Jesus this Advent season and throughout the year? How will you change the world around you? Whose life will you impact? With God's strength and help and His power working through you, there's no telling what you'll do for Him if you simply accept His love and put Him first in your life.

Dear Lord, we ask for the power of God's love to be at work in us so that we can do immeasurably more than we think or imagine. We make this prayer in Your Son's name.

Amen.

ACTIVITY

What You'll Need:
- ❈ colored paper
- ❈ scissors
- ❈ glitter
- ❈ crayons/colored pencils/markers
- ❈ string or ribbon
- ❈ hole punch
- ❈ a giving heart

During the season of Advent,

you're probably going to put up a Christmas tree. It will have lots of sparkling ornaments, some of which you've made, and lots of exciting presents waiting patiently underneath, ready to be opened on Christmas morning. This year, as you prepare for the biggest blessing of all, why not send out your own personal blessings? Pull out your craft supplies and make some more ornaments—prayer ornaments. Cut out the best shapes you can—Mom and Dad can help—and write down prayers for all the people you love and all the people in the whole entire world you want to remember this Christmas. Punch a hole in the top and tie up some string or ribbon so that all the good things in your heart can decorate your home.

Christmas is all about spreading joy and light, so what better way to celebrate Christ's coming than to hang up your own prayers right beside the twinkling lights of your tree! You can also pass the blessings on by attaching these personalized prayer ornaments to gifts for friends and family.

This is how we know what love is: Jesus Christ laid down his life for us. And we ought to lay down our lives for our brothers. If anyone has material possessions and sees his brother in need but has no pity on him, how can the love of God be in him? Dear children, let us not love with words or tongue but with actions and in truth. This then is how we know that we belong to the truth, and how we set our hearts at rest in his presence whenever our hearts condemn us. For God is greater than our hearts, and he knows everything.

1 John 3:16–20

It's not always easy to help the people who need us. Sometimes we don't know what to do, or we don't feel strong enough to provide for others. But in spite our shortcomings, God knows our hearts and our good intentions, and He assures us that He will empower us to help others in need.

Imagine you are decorating your Christmas tree. You wrap the lights around and around, covering the branches. But without plugging the string of lights into the wall outlet, they won't come on, and the tree will be dark. Only when you connect the lights to the source of energy can you light up the tree.

That's how helping others works too. We have to stay connected to Jesus, the source of power and love, and allow that energy to wrap around everyone in our lives, decorating them with the grace of God. God's power enables us to love with more than words. With His help, we are able to follow through with actions and meet the needs of others, putting their needs above our own.

And that's what God's love looks like: selflessly helping others. When we stay connected to Him and His love, we are able to serve and love people the way He loves.

Dear Christ Jesus, we ask
You to embrace us with Your
powerful love so that we may
love others with words and
actions. In Your holy name
we pray. *Amen.*

Did you know?

Christmas wasn't officially celebrated on December 25 until nearly four hundred years after the birth of Christ! Bishop Liberus of Rome declared the date in 354 AD. No one really knows if December 25 is the actual date of Christ's birthday, although plenty of people have tried to figure it out. Some people say that the day the Virgin Mary became pregnant with Jesus was the same day He died years later. We know the crucifixion happened on March 25, so if Mary became pregnant on March 25, she probably would have given birth around December 25, nine months later. This is called the "Calculation Hypothesis" because there are so many numbers. Other people claim that December 25 is the right day because it falls during the time of the winter solstice, the longest night of the year, when we most need the greatest light ever to come into the world. This is called the "History of Religions Theory" because so many other people in the world celebrate and call for the gift of life at this time of the year.

There are all kinds of explanations as to why December 25 might be the right day to celebrate Christmas, but the truth is that we don't know for sure whether it's correct at all! What matters, of course, is that we take time to welcome Jesus into our world—and continue to celebrate Him every day of the year.

Thursday

And so we know and rely on the love God has for us. God is love. Whoever lives in love lives in God, and God in him. In this way, love is made complete among us so that we will have confidence on the day of judgment, because in this world we are like him. There is no fear in love. But perfect love drives out fear, because fear has to do with punishment. The one who fears is not made perfect in love.

1 John 4:16–18

There are two things we need to know in order to understand God's love. The first thing is, God is love. It is in His very nature to be loving toward us as His children. And the second, we ourselves only know how to love because He loved us first.

When we understand those two things, we can perform acts of pure kindness, not because we feel we have to, but because we want to from a spirit of God's perfect love. In fact, our love for others is a sign that God lives in us. And when we allow God's love to shine in our lives, people can see the unseen God at work, and that brings Him glory, honor, and praise.

Genuine love is evidence that God is in us and has saved us. And with God's love and salvation comes the confidence that we will live forever with Him for all eternity.

Dear Savior, we thank You for Your perfect love that allows people to see God in us and desire to have a relationship with You. In Your name we pray. *Amen.*

ACTIVITY

What You'll Need:
* cards
* envelopes
* stamps
* pens
* list of addresses of family and friends

Ever wonder why we send cards during Christmastime?

Well, in 1843 an English businessman named Sir Henry Cole just didn't have enough time to write out notes of Christmas greetings to his friends. So instead, he had an artist named John Calcott Horsley design a card to have printed. And that's how the Christmas card was born!

Even today, with computers and printers and e-mail, it can take a lot of time to get our Christmas greetings sent. Sometimes it takes a little teamwork. So this week, get your family team together and begin Operation Seasons Greetings to get your cards ready to mail. If you plan ahead, you can have a family photo taken to include inside, or you can make a custom card that expresses your family's unique personality.

One person can sign the family member's names, or you can pass the cards around so that each member can write their name and a short note. When everything is ready, start an assembly line to address and lick the envelopes, then stick on the return-address labels and stamps.

When your Christmas cards are safely tucked inside a mailbox, you can all exchange high fives on a job well done!

If I speak in the tongues of men and of angels, but have not love, I am only a resounding gong or a clanging cymbal. If I have the gift of prophecy and can fathom all mysteries and all knowledge, and if I have a faith that can move mountains, but have not love, I am nothing. If I give all I possess to the poor and surrender my body to the flames, but have not love, I gain nothing. Love is patient, love is kind. It does not envy, it does not boast, it is not proud. It is not rude, it is not self-seeking, it is not easily angered, it keeps no record of wrongs. Love does not delight in evil but rejoices with the truth. It always protects, always trusts, always hopes, always perseveres.

1 Corinthians 13:1–7

This week of Advent, we've looked at the sacrificial love of God and how to become part of the holy family. We've learned that the gift of salvation through grace opens our eyes to God's love for the first time, and that as we walk with Him, He fills us with His Spirit. His powerful presence then overflows unto others so they may see God though our acts of love. And then His love is made complete in us. But the journey doesn't end there!

We have to take it a step further and discover that even if we do great things, we accomplish nothing if we are not motivated by love. Love is what makes a difference in the world, and when God does something, His goal is love. Sometimes it's hard to understand what God is doing, and that's why we need to keep asking God to work through us and help us understand His loving ways. The Bible says that if we ask, we will receive, and if we knock, the door will be opened to us (Matthew 7:7). We need to ask, seek, and knock at the door of this divine love, and it will be opened to us. Then His love will fill us so much that we will literally see God's hand at work around us today.

Dear Heavenly Father, we so need to see Your love at work in our world! We humbly pray for this awesome gift. We make this prayer in Christ's name.

Amen.

TIME MACHINE

ALL SYSTEMS ARE GO

In our time machine today, folks! Grab a seat, because we're headed to the Far East! Clear prop, and we're off!

We're soaring over the great Atlantic Ocean. We're blasting through hundreds of miles of space and time, right past croissants in France and Vikings in Scandinavia and snow in Switzerland. Hold on! We're starting to descend. That nice breeze in the clouds is getting warmer every second and it's going to be a bumpy landing on all those rocks.

Oops! Sorry for our little tumble, but look up, because we've arrived at the other side of the world and here comes what we traveled all this way to see. Can you spot that group of men on the horizon? They have been traveling for months, following a very bright star in the night sky. That's right, it's the Magi on their way to Bethlehem! But can you count how many of them there are? It's a bit fuzzy, isn't it?

The truth is, we actually don't know how many Magi there were. In ancient artwork they sometimes appear as twelve astronomers, and sometimes just two. We also don't know if they were really kings, but we do know that they were definitely wise. They knew all about science and poetry, art and religion; they would have made calendars, tracked the tides of the ocean, created medicine, and, of course, studied the night sky. So it's no surprise that King Herod called upon these men to explain the mysterious new star in the heavens.

The Gospel tells us that the Magi presented three gifts to the Christ child, which is why we tend to think there were three wise men—one for each gift. Look! The caravan is getting closer. Can you see what gifts they're carrying? Or maybe you can remember what the Bible tells us. If you said gold, frankincense, and myrrh, you've been paying attention. But what are all those things?

Well, gold is pretty straightforward. We definitely know what it looks like. And at this time in history, it would have been molded into an object or made into coins. When the Magi presented this wealth to Jesus, it symbolized His place as the one true King.

The other two gifts, frankincense and myrrh, were resins—hardened sap from plants—which smelled nice when burned, and were used to make holy anointing oils. These oils were needed in many religious ceremonies and symbolized Christ's role as priest to the world.

We may not know how many wise men were traveling in that caravan, and we may not even know how old Jesus was when they finally arrived, but we do know that they came hundreds and hundreds of miles to bring three particular gifts to the Son of God. As you're giving your own gifts this Christmas season, remember that each one can mean something very special.

Saturday

Love never fails. But where there are prophecies, they will cease; where there are tongues, they will be stilled; where there is knowledge, it will pass away. For we know in part and we prophesy in part, but when perfection comes, the imperfect disappears. When I was a child, I talked like a child, I thought like a child, I reasoned like a child. When I became a man, I put childish ways behind me. Now we see but a poor reflection as in a mirror; then we shall see face to face. Now I know in part; then I shall know fully, even as I am fully known. And now these three remain: faith, hope and love. But the greatest of these is love.

1 Corinthians 13:8–13

The Greek word for love means a selfless concern for the needs of others. Real love doesn't depend on whether the person being loved is worthy or not; instead, love is a decision, an act of the will to love—yes, even the unlovable—in obedience to God's command.

We've learned this week that God is love, and love comes from God. That's why His command to love others is so important. It's also why love is the greatest of our spiritual gifts.

Love outlasts the gifts of prophesy, tongues, and knowledge. As we mature spiritually, we keep growing in our love relationship with God, all the way until we see Jesus face-to-face in heaven. Growing in His love is how we obey Him when He tells us to love our neighbor, even when our neighbor is hard to love.

May you love others as He has commanded, may you be in step with His love always, and may you seek His love above all else.

Dear Jesus, by the power of Your Spirit within us, enlighten us and empower us to love as You love. In Your name we make this prayer. *Amen.*

ACTIVITY

What You'll Need:
* loud singing voices
* extra prayer ornaments or Christmas trinkets
* lots and lots of hugs

Christmas is the most wonderful time of year

—but it can also be a very difficult time of year for people who are sick and lonely. Visiting your local nursing home is a fantastic way to spread cheer and goodwill to people who need it the most. So why don't you call up some friends or organize a few church members for a little outing?

Many nursing homes will allow you to drop in unexpectedly, but it's probably a good idea to call ahead to let them know you're coming. Tell them you'd like to sing carols to the residents, either room by room or in a group setting, and see what works best for them.

Since the residents may not have family or friends to bring them gifts, little things like prayer ornaments you've made, cards, or other Christmas trinkets will be a much appreciated gesture. Sing loudly, even if you can't sing at all! Your joyful voice will be music to their ears even if you can't carry a tune. And don't forget to give hugs before you leave. There's nothing in the world that can replace human touch, and a loving hand is healing to the soul.

Reaching out to others is an important part of the Christmas season. It's how we share the good news of Christ's birth with people in need—and the blessings we receive in turn make our own Advent even more wonderful.

This fourth week of Advent will change depending on when Christmas Eve falls in the calendar year. Remember, the end of Advent is midnight Christmas Eve, so each year you will need to begin Joy on the last Sunday before Christmas and count how many days there are until Christmas Eve. Read the daily devotions for however many days you need and end on the devotion for Christmas Eve at the end of the book. There will be some years when you will need all seven days, and some years when Christmas Eve is on a Sunday; in that case, the Christmas Eve devotion will be the only devotion for Joy that year.

You have made known to me
the path of life; you will fill
me with joy in your presence,
with eternal pleasures
at your right hand.

Psalm 16:11

Joy

Continuing further on your journey, light the three purple and the pink Advent candles together as a family.

Sunday

Send forth your light and your truth, let them
guide me; let them bring me to your holy mountain,
to the place where you dwell. Then will I go to the
altar of God, to God, my joy and my delight.
I will praise you with the harp, O God, my God.

Psalm 43:3–4

During the past weeks of Advent, we have read from the Bible and spent time talking with the Lord through prayer. His Word has taught us that He has sent His light and truth into the world to save us from our sins, and that He is faithful to care for His people. What a great God! So come, let us adore Him. Let's praise and worship Him and find great joy in His presence.

Take time each day this week to make a joyful noise! Praise and worship God through the singing of Christmas carols. Let each member of your family pick a favorite carol and sing together to Jesus, our Savior and King.

Dear Lord, we praise and
worship the King of Kings
and the Lord of Lords!
We praise Your holy name!
In Jesus' name we make
this prayer. *Amen.*

Monday

It is good to praise the LORD and make music to your name, O Most High, to proclaim your love in the morning and your faithfulness at night, to the music of the ten-stringed lyre and the melody of the harp. For you make me glad by your deeds, O LORD; I sing for joy at the works of your hands.

Psalm 92:1–4

God is continually at work in the world, and everything He does is wonderful. Take time together as a family to marvel at God's amazing creation and all the good things He does. Maybe you live where there is cold and snow at this time of year, but brave the cold and take a walk, play in the snow with your family, or turn off the TV and drink hot chocolate in front of a window while watching the snow as it softly blankets the ground in white. Wherever you live, take time to enjoy nature and appreciate God's wondrous creation.

Most of all, find joy in His salvation. For your carols today, you may want to include "Silent Night" to reflect on the beauty God has made and all the wonderful things He does in our lives.

Dear Christ Jesus, we thank You for Your wonderful creation and all the great things You have done for us. We praise You and make this prayer in Your holy name.

Amen.

Fun fact

Did you ever wonder what in the world all the strange characters in the song "The Twelve Days of Christmas" have to do with Christmas? What's with all of the birds and leaping lords? It's actually more than a silly song—it's a secret code!

From 1558 until 1829, Roman Catholics in England were not allowed to practice their faith. In fact, being Catholic was a crime! So to preserve their teaching and doctrine, someone wrote this carol as a catechism song for young Catholics. It has a hidden meaning known only to members of their church. Each element in the carol has a code word for a religious reality, which the children could remember.

❄ A partridge in a pear tree represented Jesus Christ.

❄ Two turtle doves were the Old and New Testaments.

❄ Three French hens stood for faith, hope, and love.

❄ Four calling birds were the four gospels: Matthew, Mark, Luke, and John.

❄ Five golden rings recalled the Torah or Law, the first five books of the Old Testament.

❄ Six geese a-laying stood for the six days of creation.

❄ Seven swans a-swimming represented the sevenfold gifts of the Holy Spirit: prophesy, serving, teaching, exhortation, contribution, leadership, and mercy; it also represents the seven sacraments: baptism, Eucharist (or Communion), reconciliation, confirmation, marriage, holy orders, and anointing of the sick.

❄ Eight maids a-milking were the eight beatitudes.

❄ Nine ladies dancing were the nine fruits of the Holy Spirit: love, joy, peace, patience, kindness, goodness, faithfulness, gentleness, and self-control.

❄ The ten lords a-leaping were the Ten Commandments.

❄ Eleven pipers piping stood for the eleven faithful disciples.

❄ Twelve drummers drumming were symbolic of the twelve points of belief in the Apostles' Creed.

So "The Twelve Days of Christmas" isn't just a silly song after all!

Tuesday

> Be joyful always; pray continually;
> give thanks in all circumstances, for this
> is God's will for you in Christ Jesus.
>
> 1 Thessalonians 5:16–18

Lots of events in life make us happy: births, graduations, weddings, achieving something we worked hard for. But there are other circumstances—things like sickness, money problems, trouble with our relationships, or the death of someone we love—that bring deep sadness and fear. If bad things are happening around us, how can we be joyful always?

The joy deep within our hearts doesn't always show up as laughter and happiness. The joy that comes from what Christ has done for us constantly fills our hearts; it doesn't depend on the circumstances of our lives.

We can choose to be joyful even when life is difficult the same way we choose to love those who are seemingly unlovable: by an act of our will. We do this by focusing on Christ instead of the situation that's going on in our life. This isn't easy, but it's certainly not impossible. The Bible is full of examples of people who found joy in the midst of the worst situations, and if we look around, we'll see other examples all around us.

You have the ability through Christ to choose to fill your heart with joy. Praise and worship Jesus in song as you sing your carols today.

Take turns today letting each family member lift up his or her own personal prayers to God. Speak whatever is on your heart, and remember to make your prayer in Christ's name.

ACTIVITY

What You'll Need:
❈ construction paper
❈ colored pencils
❈ crayons
❈ markers
❈ glue or paste
❈ stickers
❈ glitter
❈ ribbon
❈ small boxes or jars

Everyone loves to open Christmas presents, right?

But as much as we like to peel off the wrapping paper to reveal something fun and new and unexpected, the very best presents are the simplest—the ones that simply say "I love you." So get everyone in your family together, spread out your craft supplies, and make some Christmas coupons to share with each other.

Each person should have their own jar or box. Before you get started, draw names so each person has another family member's name. Cut out small squares of paper, decorate each piece, and write your "gift" on it. For example, if you pick your mom, a gift she might enjoy would be eight big hugs, or cleaning your room without complaining. Dad might like help with cleaning the garage or shoveling snow, and siblings might like for you to play games with them or help them with their chores. Fill your designated family member's box with these coupons for services that you will willingly and lovingly do when the coupon is presented back to you.

Decorate your boxes and put them in a safe place until Christmas Eve. And get ready for a whole year full of simple, sweet presents!

Wednesday

> Therefore, since we are surrounded by such a great cloud of witnesses, let us throw off everything that hinders and the sin that so easily entangles, and let us run with perseverance the race marked out for us. Let us fix our eyes on Jesus, the author and perfecter of our faith, who for the joy set before him endured the cross, scorning its shame, and sat down at the right hand of the throne of God. Consider him who endured such opposition from sinful men, so that you will not grow weary and lose heart.

> Hebrews 12:1–3

The Bible describes our spiritual journey as a long-distance race, not a short sprint! We've got a long course to run so if we're going to achieve our goal—the joy of being together with Jesus in heaven—we have to focus on Him and keep pressing on.

Our faith began with Christ and will be completed in Him. He is the beginning and the end, the Alpha and the Omega. He has already overcome. When we think about these truths, we find new energy to keep going, and we can't help but be joyful.

So stand firm, take hold of joy, don't grow weary, remember the "cloud of witnesses"—the disciples, the apostles, and the saints who have gone on before us—and finish the journey! Sing a song of praise today, knowing that God has already provided victory for us, and that He continually gives us strength each step of the way.

Dear Heavenly Father, we pray for willing and joyful spirits to sustain us and help us to finish the race and not lose heart. We make this prayer in Christ's name. *Amen.*

Did you know?

There are nine different kinds of angels, but they all have something in common—they are all messengers of God. The word *angel* actually comes from the Greek word *angelos*, meaning *messenger*. In fact, angels are often depicted wearing halos, and just as the circular shape of the Advent wreath reminds us of God's love that has no end and no beginning, the halo symbolizes the connection between God's ever-lasting wisdom and His almighty will that's to be carried out by the angels.

But even though angels all share the same mission, each category of angels has a different set of honors and duties, so we classify them into nine levels of hierarchy. From the lowest to the highest order, the classes are: angel, virtue, archangel, power, principality, minion, throne, cherub, and seraph.

During Advent we focus on one particular archangel who God chose to deliver the Annunciation to the Virgin Mary. Even though he was only in the third out of the nine classifications, God chose the Archangel Gabriel to bring the first news of Jesus to the world. Lesson learned: no matter what category or hierarchy we fall into, no matter what our age or experience or responsibilities, God uses us and gives us the strength to do things much greater than we could imagine!

May the nations be glad and sing for joy, for you rule the peoples justly and guide the nations of the earth. Selah. May the peoples praise you, O God; may all the peoples praise you. Then the land will yield its harvest, and God, our God, will bless us. God will bless us, and all the ends of the earth will fear him.

Psalm 67:4–7

In Luke 2:30–32, a wise man named Simeon rejoiced over the baby Jesus: "My eyes have seen your salvation, which you have prepared in the sight of all people, a light for revelation to the Gentiles and for glory to your people Israel." Simeon recognized in the tiny baby Jesus that God had come to earth to save the whole world from our sins.

Jesus is the light of the world and He has given us the responsibility of sharing His light with the world around us. Let us praise the Lord for His great blessings and mercies, and let us honor Him with all our good deeds in such a way that we share the news of God's love with everyone we meet.

For one of your carols today, you may want to sing, "Joy to the World." With joy in our hearts, let's catch the attentions of the nations and bring God worldwide praise.

Dear Jesus, we thank You and praise You for all You bring into our lives; help us to be ever mindful of Your daily blessings. In Your name we make this prayer. *Amen.*

ACTIVITY

Grab some Christmas music, a few snacks, and those favorite games—it's game night!

Tonight, take some time to simply enjoy each other's company as a family. Press "pause" on all of the wrapping, baking, and shopping, and just sit down to be together and have fun. You'll feel less stressed and have a good time—and make a priceless Christmas memory.

Sing to the LORD a new song, for he has done marvelous things; his right hand and his holy arm have worked salvation for him. The LORD has made his salvation known and revealed his righteousness to the nations. He has remembered his love and his faithfulness to the house of Israel; all the ends of the earth have seen the salvation of our God. Shout for joy to the LORD, all the earth, burst into jubilant song with music; make music to the LORD with the harp, with the harp and the sound of singing, with trumpets and the blast of the ram's horn—shout for joy before the LORD, the King.

Psalm 98:1–6

Rejoice in our King! When we sing our worship to the Lord, as we have been doing all week with our carols, we commune with Him in an expression of ultimate joy. The notes lift our words to the Word, the melody exalts our souls to the Spirit, and we are united in the faith we will share to the ends of the earth.

Praise God, who saves us from our sins! Praise God, who brings us comfort and strength and joy! He is worthy of our praise, and as we praise Him, we invite others to do so as well, and we "make disciples of all nations" (Matthew 28:19). The joy of the Lord is one of so many blessings of Christmas. Make this Christmas an occasion for praise.

Dear Lord, we praise You for salvation; help us share with others what You have done for us. In Your Son's name we pray.

Amen.

TIME MACHINE

IT'S TIME to rev up our time machine for one last trip! Hold on tight because this turbo boost is gonna knock your socks off. Now watch how this machine can corner!

My fellow passengers, welcome to Bethlehem—which means "house of bread" in Hebrew—on the eve of Christ's birth. The Bethlehem that exists in modern day Israel is a very different place from what you see before you. Take a look around. The little town is nestled between the deserts of the East and the farmland of the West. Those forests of pine trees will later be cut down by the Romans, but the pastures over that hill where you can see the shepherds and their flocks roaming are still there today, and are still the home of modern-day shepherds. The town is so small it might be called a village. Only between three hundred to a thousand people live here, most of whom are stonemasons, wheat farmers, livestock keepers, and weavers. Take a moment and listen to how still and peaceful this place is. What a perfect place for Jesus to come into the world.

Well, folks, we've traveled far and wide in our time machine, to the lands of Ancient Greece and Egypt, to deserts and cities across the earth, to see the birth of a Word, a light, and a journey. And all of these led us to our last stop here in Bethlehem, on our own journey to the tranquil place where our Savior was born into the world by the grace of God!

Christmas Eve

Light all the Advent
candles and the white
Christ candle together
as a family.

> This is how the birth of Jesus Christ came about: His mother Mary was pledged to be married to Joseph, but before they came together, she was found to be with child through the Holy Spirit.
>
> Matthew 1:18

Divide the verses in Luke 2:1–20 so that each family member can read aloud.

Now read the story of the birth of our Savior together.

We've journeyed through Scripture this Advent season, learning about God's wonderful gifts to us at Christmas. Remember each Sunday of Advent represents the four comings of Christ. The first Sunday is His coming in the flesh, His birth, which you will celebrate tomorrow. The Second is His coming into the hearts of all who believe in Him. The third is His coming at the hour of death to all who know Him as Lord and Savior, and the fourth is His coming at the Final Judgment.

As you sit together in front of your Advent wreath with all of the lit candles, say a prayer of thanksgiving to God for the gift of His Son. Thank Him for sending Jesus to save the world from our sins. Thank Jesus for knowing us and carrying all of our burdens. And as you prepare to start a new year, choose to celebrate this great gift of Jesus each day, relying on Him to light your way out into the world as you share His love with others.